MARTIN LUTHER KING, JR.

MARTIN LUTHER KING, JR.

Text by Robert G. Hoyt

Published by

Country Beautiful Foundation, Inc., Waukesha, Wisconsin

Distributed by RAND McNALLY & COMPANY

Publisher and Editorial Director: Michael P. Dineen; *Executive Editor:* Robert L. Polley; *Senior Editors:* Kenneth L. Schmitz, James H. Robb; *Art Director:* Wilbur Howe; *Editorial Assistants:* Carolyn Muchhala, Lawrence Kenney, Janice M. Puta; *Executive Director, Sales and Marketing:* Richard W. Stone; *Production:* Frank Bruce; *Circulation Manager:* Trudy Schnittka; *Administrative Secretary:* Donna Griesemer; *Editorial Secretaries:* Christine Maynard, Darcy Davies.

The editors would like to thank the following publishers for permission to reprint sections from their books:

By permission of Joan Daves and Harper & Row
Copyright © 1957, 1960 by Martin Luther King, Jr., Estate
Copyright © 1964 by the Nobel Foundation

From:
STRIDE TOWARD FREEDOM
WHY WE CAN'T WAIT
WHERE DO WE GO FROM HERE: CHAOS OR COMMUNITY?
Published by Harper & Row
Copyright © 1958, 1963, 1964, 1967 by Martin Luther King, Jr.

From:
BEHIND THE SELMA MARCH
Copyright © 1965 by Martin Luther King, Jr.

CONTENTS

Preface

The voice of Martin Luther King, Jr., has been stilled; his message must still be heard. That is the point of this book. It is not a biography, nor is it only a memorial tribute. It is offered, rather, as an occasion for reflective listening.

When that murderous news came from Memphis many Americans, including the editor of this volume, experienced not only grief and shock but also a sense of shame. We had sympathized with him, we admired his zeal and courage, we hoped for his success. Sometimes, as on the occasion of the momentous "I Have a Dream" address of the 1963 March on Washington, we let ourselves be exalted by the sweep of his rhetoric and the nobility of his vision. But when the rifle spoke and he fell, in that instant we could measure the depth of our devotion to the good cause he led. Here, beyond dispute, was a great man who fought for justice by pure means. Even more significantly, here was a teacher who shaped a doctrine and developed a technique capable of revolutionizing the earth. Confronted with this greatness, we cut it to our measure; we gave him half our attention. When the bullet struck, we felt shame because we knew it was too late to give the response he had merited.

This book is an effort to defeat the purpose of the assassin. Its thesis is that we are still in the age of Martin Luther King: We face the same situation he worked to understand and change; the ideas he offered are alive and relevant. His place in history cannot be fixed be- cause we are still choosing the place to give him in our minds and hearts. He can still shape the history we are making – provided we listen.

At some risk of trivialization, the book can be thought of as a printed version of television's "instant replay" device, which permits viewers to focus again, and more closely, on a bit of climactic action in the course of a sports event. The comparison is apt not only because the whole career of the book's subject was a decisive moment in the flux of American history, but because the ideas to be focused on here were developed in the midst of action and conflict. Dr. King was fully capable of detached scholarly analysis, but in fact his doctrine came into being to meet the needs of crisis. Accordingly, much of the book's content is made up of the words he spoke in moments of high tension: in news conferences, at rallies, in interviews. The photographs accompanying the text will convey some sense of the urgent immediacies in the midst of which he sought to frame a permanently valid rationale for social revolution. This accompanying commentary is meant to supply relevant factual material and to offer a degree of interpretation.

From what has already been said, it will be obvious that the interpretation is not neutral or uncommitted toward Dr. King; the book is published in furtherance of his cause. At the same time, it is not an exercise in myth-making. He was a man among men, not a demigod; limited, fallible, capable of confusion and failure; possibly a saint, probably not a genius; able to inspire great masses to great acts of courage, and yet not universal in his appeal. But he did not ask adulation, and neither does this book ask it for him. He wanted and deserved a hearing. — Robert G. Hoyt

Thomas Harris

8

I Years of Preparation

Martin Luther King, Jr., was born in Atlanta, Georgia, on January 29, 1929. His father was a respected Baptist minister and community leader; so also was his mother's father, the Reverend A. D. Williams. The boy Martin grew up in secure and even comfortable circumstances, though like any other Southern Negro child, he early encountered — and raged against — the mysterious, demeaning reality of segregation. An able and diligent student, he entered Morehouse College in Atlanta at the age of fifteen. At that time, repelled by the emotionalism and lack of social relevance in the Southern Negro church, he was determined to be a lawyer but in his junior year, under the influence of Dr. Benjamin E. Mays, President of Morehouse, he formed a new conception of the ministry which matched his talents and aspirations. In 1947, even before graduation, he was ordained and became assistant pastor of his father's Ebenezer Baptist Church.

In 1948, King entered Crozer Theological Seminary in Chester, Pennsylvania, where he was one of six Negro students in a student body of one hundred. He received the bachelor of divinity degree in 1951; he was president of his class, its "most outstanding student," and recipient of a fellowship for graduate study. His graduate work was done in the department of systematic theology at Boston University. During these years, he met and courted Coretta Scott, a native of Heiberger, Alabama, a graduate of Antioch College in Yellow Springs, Ohio, and a student (when King met her) at the New England Conservatory of Music. They were married June 18, 1953. The following year, having completed his course work at the university, King accepted a call to become pastor of the Dexter Avenue Baptist Church in Montgomery, Alabama. (He completed his doctoral thesis and received his Ph. D. degree after assuming his pastoral duties.)

The choice of Montgomery was a highly deliberate one; King could have had a Northern pastorate or an academic post. It was also a fateful choice, for it placed him at the center of events when a tiny incident on a Montgomery city bus sparked an all-but-spontaneous protest movement in the Negro community. It was largely by an accident of history that he was thrust into leadership of the 382-day bus boycott that followed. Under the pressure of events, responding both to his own temperament and to ideas developed during his long studies, King created a rationale — the first outline of his philosophy of non-violence that both sustained the morale of the movement and gave it a significance transcending by far the immediate local issues. By his conduct during those 382 days, King laid the foundation for national and world fame. At the same time, as *Newsweek* put it thirteen years later, he took the first step of his march toward martyrdom.

In a sense the martyrdom began immediately. During the boycott he experienced his first arrest, first jailing and first conviction; his home was bombed and his family endangered. Perhaps even harder to bear was the burden of leadership put upon him. At the age of twenty-seven he was suddenly a foremost spokesman for the largest and most restless minority in the country. Reared in the quiet security of a middle-class home, trained chiefly in the analysis of ideas, gifted primarily with a power of conceptualization and articulation, he now bore the central responsibility for direction of an activist mass movement. As he well knew, his background and talents did not mesh perfectly with the requirements of his role. He compensated for his deficiencies as administrator and tactician by hard work and by relentlessly exploiting his assets. He wrote, lectured, traveled widely, gave interviews and news conferences, sat in on innumerable strategy meetings. In a single year, he logged nearly 800,000 miles and delivered 208 speeches.

In that same post-boycott period, he completed the manuscript of his first book, *Stride Toward Freedom*; visited India and Ghana; helped organize and became the first president of the Southern Christian Leadership Conference; conferred with Vice-President Nixon and President Eisenhower; and suffered a near-fatal stabbing. All this while he struggled with a formidable intellectual task: to deepen his own grasp of Gandhi's *satyagraha*, to weld it to his own understanding of the Christian Gospel, to invent tactics for its application in the circumstances of the Negro revolution, to find a style for its presentation that would appeal both to the profoundly religious Negro masses in the South and to the pragmatic, secularized, skeptical liberals, white and black, of the North.

This creative task had to be accomplished in an incredibly fluid situation. Partly because of King's own success, partly because of a larger tide of events, the civil rights movement underwent one metamorphosis after another; and each time the stakes and the tension rose higher. With every small advance for black Americans, the mood of white America shifted from sympathy toward fear and resistance. These same small gains helped Negroes realize more profoundly the distance they had to travel to achieve real equality. White backlash nurtured black cynicism; new doctrines and new leaders challenged King and his non-violent approach. "Freedom Now!" was an irritant to whites, who did not understand or would not acknowledge that Negroes were still enslaved; but to black militants and nationalists it was neither real enough nor explosive enough. They wanted "Black Power!"

It is beyond the scope of this book to chronicle in detail the events that led from Montgomery to Memphis. During the period of the sit-ins and freedom rides King was, at most, an adviser on tactics and strategy, but as interpreter-ideologist-spokesman he was at the forefront. The first effort by the Southern Christian Leadership Conference to confront and overcome a local segregationist power structure came at Albany, Georgia. It ended in failure. But then, in April 1963, King launched a massive, well-prepared campaign for specific, significant racial goals in Birmingham, Alabama. Birmingham Safety Commissioner "Bull" Connor played into the hands of the demonstrators by his use of fire hoses and police dogs, even against children. Connor's savagery sickened the nation; more importantly, it spelled out before the world the fanaticism with which defenders of the "Southern way of life" clung to the privilege of exploiting the Negro caste. With thousands of demonstrators packed into the jails, King kept up the pressure. Shamed before the world, facing the imminent possibility of wholesale social disorganization, the white community gave in and appointed a committee to negotiate an agreement, which was announced during the second week of May.

Though in the perspective of later events its significance has faded, Birmingham was a famous victory. It brought King very near the pinnacle of his career, and no doubt had a part in his selection to receive the Nobel Prize in the following year. It helped convert John F. Kennedy into a true believer and gave impetus to eventual passage of the Civil Rights Act of 1964. It produced a new classic of prison literature, King's "Letter from a Birmingham Jail." And it made King the focus of anticipation at the 1963 March on Washington. There, speaking from the steps of the Lincoln Memorial to an enormous crowd, he described his vision of a free and brotherly America in the most burningly eloquent statement of his public life.

For a time, the critics of non-violence were silenced; but only for a time. And that was inevitable. However symbolic and promising, the victory at Birmingham was local and limited. However hard-fought the legislative battle that brought the Civil Rights Act to passage, the result was words on paper — words still not fully implemented in policy or in the courts, and words that for the most part did not touch the economic realities of Negro life in the urban ghettos and rural slums. Something similar could be said of the last great triumph registered by King and the SCLC, the Selma-Montgomery march and its sequel, the civil rights act of 1965. The drama was exhilarating, the victory was real, the results were significant — but not significant enough. Guaranteed access to the ballot — provided the guarantee held up in practice — held promise for the future; it did not bring the fullness of freedom now, much less the realization of black power. And, when King turned his attention to the cities of the North, he encountered opponents far wilier than Birmingham's "Bull" Connor or Selma's Jim Clark, rivalries much fiercer than the factionalism of the Southern Negro establishment. The campaigns in Chicago and elsewhere had the value of revealing the depths of bigotry in the enlightened, liberal North. In King's eyes that was no small value, because the cancer had to be known before it could be cured. There were more tangible gains as well. But there were no Selmas.

Worst of all, just as blacks (including King) and some few of their white allies had begun to realize with full intensity the true scope of America's racial and urban crisis, and the necessity of a "Marshall Plan" or a "Freedom Budget" to deal with it, there came the escalation of the Vietnam War. "The bombs that fall in Vietnam," said Martin Luther King, "are exploding at home; they destroy the hopes and possibilities for a decent America." They seemed also to destroy the last hope that Americans in any significant numbers would ever achieve a mature understanding of non-violence. King never meant non-violence to be a mere tactic; for him its validity depended on its inner truth, not on its success of the moment. But in America, truth is apt to be measured on a scorecard.

This falling note characterized most of the journalistic accounts of Martin Luther King's career written at the time of his death by assassination, April 4, 1968. Given the assumptions of journalism, its self-imposed restriction to a superficial factuality, it was fair enough to suggest that King's message had had its day; that is the way it looked. But the same judgment had been passed many times in his lifetime; each time the buried doctrine rose from its grave and inspired a new army of believers. It can be argued, of course, that it was King's own faith and his charismatic presence that brought about these improbable resurrections. That, however, is a proposition that can be tested by time. After King's death, the ideas that shaped his life had the power to sustain his followers in the Poor People's Campaign, in the building of Resurrection City, in the staging of the Solidarity Day March of June 1968, and the march to Atlanta in May 1970 protesting Negro deaths in Augusta and Jackson State College. The ideas are still available for inspection. At one or another level of understanding, they exist in the minds of millions of men and women who learned from King while he lived. The seeds of his doctrine are present also in this book; may they find good ground.

II Prophet of Justice and Love

For some readers the chapter title may have misleading connotations. In certain contexts "prophet" suggests a visionary who claims to see the future, and in some usages words like "justice" and "love" have a softness about them. Given that flavoring of the words, a prophet of justice and love would be someone who spreads good cheer and urges everyone to be nice.

Martin Luther King was not soft, nor was he a pseudo-mystic seer. He was a prophet in the root scriptural meaning of the term, in the tradition of Amos and Jeremiah: a man who sees very plainly the moral condition of the human community and describes it in harsh, burning words. The work of the prophet so understood is not only to hold up lofty ideals of goodness but to pinpoint evil — particularly the insidious evils of injustice and hypocrisy — and to fix responsibility.

The specific evil King fought was, of course, American racism, a phenomenon both simple and infinitely complex, at once blatant and endlessly subtle. Probably no one could catalogue all the ramifications of structured racism, and there will always be debate about what constitutes its essential core. But during the course of his public career King delivered an acute and devastating analysis of racial persecution in the United States, a powerfully persuasive indictment that was accepted by many who had never been moved or even reached by other critics of racism.

There were many reasons for his effectiveness. King spoke

Thomas Harris

of the hurt of black Americans out of his own hurt; from childhood he knew that to have a dark skin in a racist society was to be an unshielded target for hatred and contempt. He was a brilliant man, apt in absorbing facts and ordering them for maximum effect. He was a born rhetorician, master of the vivid phrase, the telling comparison, the moving example drawn from life; and he was an artful speaker with a rich and ranging baritone voice.

But these gifts were not unique, even in combination. Two factors set King apart and made him a prophet rather than only a social critic or a pressure group leader: the nobility of his character and the nature of his message. Except for determined bigots, it was really very hard for anyone not to see that King was a good man. Even people who found personal goodness rather stuffy felt his attraction. Secondly, what he taught reflected what he was. He could be as passionate as any black nationalist in his attacks on racial oppression; there was no questioning the depth and honesty of his moral outrage. But he attacked the structure of racism rather than its agents, the system rather than the persons who ran it; not because he had illusions about the viciousness and ferocity of racists, but because in fighting them he refused to become like them. More will be said of this in the next chapter; the point to be stressed here is that his intellectual system was at one with his character and exerted the same magnetism.

On the face of things, King was improbably cast for his role. In looking about for a man to become a major prophet to twentieth-century America, one would not choose a twenty-five-year-old black minister, pastor of the Dexter Avenue Baptist Church in Montgomery, Alabama. Not many Americans want their clergymen to be prophets; at least until very recently, not many clergymen have felt called upon to exceed the expectations of the culture. Yet King always insisted that he was first of all a pastor, a minister of Christ's Gospel. His race was, of course, the condition of his special apostolate, but it was also (again: of course) the main source of his problems in reaching the holders of social power; for if Americans have a selective filter for screening out excessively pertinent clerical criticisms, they have all-channel earplugs to keep from hearing the voices of black men. Finally, King was not only a Negro but a Southern Negro. The lilt of the Gospel shouter could be heard even in his most erudite addresses, a reminder for many of a tradition they had rejected or never shared.

To an extent, King turned these liabilities into assets. He simply over-leaped the wall insulating sacred from secular, the clerical caste from the affairs of "real life." In doing so he multiplied his own power, for his example made the prophetic vocation once more a live option — first among young Southern Negro ministers like himself, then more broadly. He overcame the handicap of blackness because he did not experience it as a handicap. He was at ease in a black skin, and his self-respect made itself felt like a natural force. And, if traces of the Southern Negro tradition turned off some of his hearers, that same tradition was indispensable in building his base of power.

When the direct action phase of the Negro revolution began at Montgomery, Alabama, in 1955, its focus was on the human dignity of the black person, outraged by the caste system of segregation. Critics said free access to public transportation and to lunch counters didn't help a black man who didn't have the price of a bus ticket or a hamburger because his blackness kept him from getting a job. Acknowledging the measure of truth in this, King argued that the assertion of selfhood through mass non-violent rejection of the symbols of segregation was the first thing necessary. Only when blacks had learned they could demand and get recognition as full human persons would they be ready to attack the foundations of the system — discrimination in jobs, politics, education, housing and every other phase of life. But this could be a rationale imposed by hindsight; there may be more immediate reasons explaining why King could respond instantly and with all his soul to the issues at stake in the bus boycott. The rules of the caste system on buses, at train and air terminals, in stores and restaurants applied quite as harshly to the brilliant young minister with his Ph.D. as to the hod carrier or the seamstress. Moreover, by temperament and in his formal philosophy King was a personalist, unusually sensitive to the profound, intolerable implications of enforced apartheid, of "whites only" and "colored only" signs on drinking fountains and restroom doors.

Whatever the explanation, certainly there is a progression to be observed over the years in King's social analysis (and that of his colleagues and rivals in the movement): from symbolic issues to gut issues, from civil rights to the full range of human rights, and finally to war and peace. Whether or not the range of his awareness broadened, the sophistication of his critique deepened. Though King was a

Robert Fitch (Black Star)

sociology major at Morehouse before deciding on the ministry, the study of social reality was far from being the focus of his graduate studies, which were concentrated rather on abstract philosophical and theological themes. (His Ph.D. thesis was entitled "A Comparison of the Conceptions of God in the Thinking of Paul Tillich and Henry Nelson Wieman.") If he was not self-taught, certainly as prophet of social justice he was self-developed. Yet he entered into detailed dissection of "The System" with ease and confidence. When he wrote of job discrimination, the welfare system, education and housing, his values were always very much present to the analysis, but there was never any sense of the preacher moralizing in the absence of the facts.

Though King was often denounced as a radical and an extremist, in fact his social philosophy was conventional rather than original, essentially reformist rather than revolutionary. Basically he accepted the status quo in America, both its pressure-group politics and its mixed capitalist-socialist economics. All that he asked (or, better, demanded) was that the benefits and opportunities of the system be extended fairly to all. He refused to develop or swallow a mystique of "negritude" — blackness was beautiful, but not more beautiful than whiteness. So far as social structure is concerned, he appealed not to novel doctrines but to established Christian and democractic traditions. What made him radical was that he believed them. What made him original was that he found in nonviolence a way of insisting that the country practice its own preachments.

III Gandhi in America

The cause for which Martin Luther King, Jr., did his living and his dying was less significant than the means he developed in service of the cause. Granted, the race question is both morally and politically crucial, one of the three or four overriding issues of the century. But non-violence as philosophy and technique, though peculiarly applicable to racism, is not relevant only to race, or only to this century. It is inevitable and right that King will always be identified with the Negro revolution in the United States. But to focus solely on this identification might well deny him his rightful place in history. Far worse, it might deny to future history the leavening influence that a deeper understanding of his career could have on the affairs of men.

Lest these assertions seem grandiose, some qualifications are in order. The instruction "Love your enemy" had been part of man's heritage a long time before being rethought by this obscure Baptist minister. And it was not King but Mohandas K. Gandhi (in part following Thoreau) who saw that Christ's admonition might contain something more than a supreme ideal of personal perfection offered to a spiritual elite. It was Gandhi who realized that loving your enemy need not mean submitting to his oppression — that love could become the instrument of a revolutionary mass movement for social justice. Except for injecting a stronger flavoring of the Christian Gospel, King did not really add to Gandhi's basic insight, nor did he give it definitive philosophical expression. His was not a triumph of intellect but of character and charisma. There is nothing terribly abstruse or difficult about non-violence as an idea; anyone not lost to cynicism can grasp it, and a good many people practice it at least fitfully in their personal lives. Only a rare soul could live it integrally without social support; only a magnetic personality could bring it to life in a mass following. That was King's accomplishment: He made non-violence credible at a specific time in a specific setting. The setting happened to be the United States of America, a highly visible society that was at the moment incomparably influential in fixing the course of history over the entire globe. The time was one of high tension and unprecedented risk. King did not set out to be a global savior but he knew the potential that lay within his doctrine.

"Non-violence" is, of course, badly named. The term conveys only one of the key elements in the idea, and then only by negation. "Passive resistance" is unsatisfactory as well, especially to the American ear, both because the adjective seems to call for a non-virile, selfhood-denying posture and because "resistance" contains no hint of progress, of creative change. Gandhi's term, *satyagraha,* which King translated as "soul force," does suggest the tension within the concept by combining the idea of power with that of spiritualization. But the element of *mass* action for *social* change is absent — Gandhi's term is too "religious." The truth is that the idea of non-violence is complex and no sloganeering label will cover it.

In expounding non-violence in the context of the American tradition it is probably wise to put the initial stress on the goal it pursues, the establishment of justice. Far from requiring capitulation to tyrants, it presents a fierce and uncompromising demand for the fulfillment of human rights. But this end (says the theory) can be reached without violence, either the external violence of riots and warfare or the internal violence of hatred. In fact, the choice of violence as a means is not only unnecessary but wrong — and wrong not only in an ethical sense but also in the practical order. Men cannot build the "beloved community" out of hatred. The aim of non-violence, then, must not be to inflict defeat and humiliation on personal enemies but to achieve reconciliation, to make enemies into friends, to overcome evil with good.

But if good is to win over evil without relying on the weapons in evil's armory, it has to do more than celebrate its own beauty. It has to be tactically resourceful, energetic, inventive, clever and flexible. It would be a mistake, of course, to identify non-violence with the particular tactics used in the 1950's and '60's by the non-violent wing of the Negro revolution — boycotts, sit-ins, kneel-ins, mass marches and demonstrations. There are, however, strategic elements closer to the heart of the theory, elements touched on by King again and again in the course of the years. Among them:

— *Civil disobedience.* Some laws are unjust, even some laws constitutionally enacted and approved or tolerated by a majority. It is sometimes permissible, sometimes even mandatory, to disobey such laws. But the rights of society must be acknowledged, and the aim must be to change the law, not to claim a personal exemption. Therefore the law must be broken openly and the penalty accepted.

— *Mass participation*. Non-violent direct action on behalf of a tyrannized group needs to enlist its members in large numbers, partly for the sake of effectiveness but also for their own healing. By relying on themselves they acquire a sense of their own worth; by risking themselves, putting their bodies on the line, they are purified.

— *Confrontation*. "Soul force" is true force. The non-violent strategist tries to create a situation to which the power structure of established disorder must respond; a situation of tension; a situation in which the latent hostility and hatred within the oppressor must become explicit and public. The defenders of unjust privilege are forced to acknowledge the hidden premises of their system; they can no longer pretend that the system is accepted by its victims or that it preserves peace and good order.

People who have committed themselves to non-violence are not necessarily either saints or geniuses. Still, the strategy does not lend itself easily to use for selfish or trivial or aberrant purposes. Men and women do not submit themselves unarmed and unshielded, pledged against anger and retaliation, to verbal abuse and physical attack (beatings, rocks, police dogs, tear gas, fire hoses) unless sustained by a profound belief in the justice of their cause. Essentially they are appealing to the consciences of their enemies and to the judgment of mankind. It is integral to the theory that the demands be made openly. Mobs cannot tolerate the presence of cameras. Non-violent demonstrators need them.

This fact helps make explicit some of the ultimate presuppositions underlying the theory of non-violence. The theory says reality has a moral structure; men are equipped, as they are with vision, to perceive it; despite cultural differences and private perversities, mankind has its conscience in common. Further, the moral universe is on the side of justice. Not, however, in the way a gambling wheel is rigged in favor of the house; that would have nothing to do with morality. Justice prevails to the extent men choose it.

Stated thus abstractly, apart from tangible issues like poverty and segregation, non-violence is not remarkably persuasive. It gains a life on the streets it cannot have in print. It has to be believed before it can be practiced, but for most of us it has to be practiced by somebody else to be believable. It seems fortunate for humanity, especially the American branch of the family, that King understood the theory of non-violence before he had occasion to use it: that when the occasion rose he had the audacity to make a commitment to it; and that the black people of Montgomery, Alabama, had the spiritual depth to respond.

IV First Testing: Montgomery

There are a couple of difficulties in the way of acquiring an accurate appreciation of what happened in Montgomery, Alabama, from December 1, 1955, when a Negro seamstress named Rosa Parks refused to give up her bus seat to a white passenger, to December 21, 1956, when the Montgomery bus lines were integrated by order of the Supreme Court of the United States.

One problem is that the bare outlines of the story have been recalled as many times as the media have had occasion to review King's career — so that (for example) the name of Mrs. Parks is almost as familiar as that of Betsy Ross, and one has a sense of knowing all there is to know of the story. The other difficulty is that the Negro revolution has moved a very long way since 1955. Both the occasion of the bus boycott and its result, which once seemed mountainous, have dwindled to triviality when viewed exclusively from the perspective of today.

The best way to correct these impressions is to read or re-read King's book-length account of the struggle, *Stride Toward Freedom*. One of the reasons King made history was that he had a sense of history. The episode became significant because from the outset he *said* it was significant; he imbued the Negroes of Montgomery with a sense that they were bearing the burdens of centuries to come. That same persuasive force still works in retrospect in *Stride Toward Freedom*. Moreover, King had a feature writer's flair for the dramatic which makes it possible for his reader to relive those tense months of teetering between tragedy and joy. It is a story worth knowing in every detail.

Here the emphasis must be on analysis rather than narration. One of the most fascinating aspects of the Montgomery story is its quality of happenstance. King might well have accepted a pastorate or an academic post elsewhere than in Montgomery. Mrs. Parks happened to have tired feet on a day of a year when she could not any longer bear the crudely artful, deliberately degrading rules of the caste system; and she happened to be attractive, well-liked and invulnerable to character assaults. Montgomery's black community happened to have the right mix of leadership talents, and its white power structure the wrong combination of rigidity and blindness. The Supreme Court decision on school desegregation the year before had created doubt among whites and hope among blacks. Seen by hindsight, the actual sequence of events — including such apparent disasters as the bombing of King's home and his conviction on charges of organizing an illegal boycott — appears to have a design imposed by a benignly partisan power, upholding King's sometimes-desperately-held faith that for him who loves God, all things conspire to bring forth good.

But if in many respects Montgomery underscores once more the spontaneity of history — if it shows that a great social revolution is ordinarily born out of an unmanageable and unpredictable concatenation of circumstances — at the same time it highlights the element of human decisiveness in seizing upon a moment of high promise and cashing it at the reality bank. In the final analysis, Montgomery was an achievement, not a happening.

Montgomery's Negroes made history because they knew exactly — indeed, profoundly — what they were doing, and because they dredged up out of themselves the organizational skills to anticipate and meet every demand that was made on them. The second element was of course a group achievement. For example, to prolong the bus boycott beyond its first near-spontaneous days it was necessary to organize a car pool; to make it work it was necessary to create in a matter of days a traffic flow system the bus company had spent years in developing. Before the boycott seventy-five percent of the bus riders had been Negroes; to invent and administer a transportation system serving some fifty thousand persons daily, on a voluntary basis, was an extraordinary feat, requiring for its support continuous supervision, flexible scheduling, fund-raising, morale maintenance and legal defense. A seamstress occasioned the boycott, a Pullman car porter started it, the Negro ministry accepted its leadership, teachers, cab drivers, pharmacists, housewives, laborers and domestic workers took responsibility; and, despite every raw and subtle effort by the opposition to create internal dissension, the Negro community maintained all but perfect unity and discipline until the final day.

This seamless unity in large part explains the maintenance of the boycott over 382 wearying days. It must itself be explained in terms of the leadership King furnished and particularly of the ideology he supplied. The Negroes of Montgomery had always been united in their suffering and by their religious tradition, but they had never previously been able to overcome their factionalism and unite in a common effort. It was not only or primarily King's inspirational oratory that made the difference in 1955. His equipment included also his religious faith, the stock of ideas on social justice and on non-violence that he had acquired, his intellectual power and, finally, another asset less easily categorized: an ability to unite thought with action. He had to understand what he was doing before he could do it. In the earliest days of the protest, for example, the Montgomery *Advertiser* published a story suggesting that the proposed boycott was a black version of coercive tactics being used by the White Citizens Councils. Instead of dismissing the charge, King took it seriously and was disturbed by it. Knowing that a good end could not justify use of evil means, he had to penetrate to the core of what was being done before he could proceed. Eventually, as he wrote, "I came to see that what we were really doing was withdrawing our cooperation from an evil system, rather than merely withdrawing our economic support from the bus company." To ride the buses in mute acceptance of the company's insulting regulations and practices was to cooperate in evil; to stay off the buses, despite the coercion involved, was right so long as the aim was to put justice into business rather than to drive the company out of business. He related this insight to Thoreau's *Essay on Civil Disobedience*. He realized, too, that by failing to protest the system he and other Negroes of the city were permitting their oppressors to continue unchecked in their oppression and all but unconscious of the evil they were imposing.

To a merely practical man this would have seemed a pointless exercise in hair-splitting. To King it was a necessity. And that moment of conscientious reflection had much to do with the shape of the protest and with its eventual success.

The first day of the movement was its most decisive one, its "day of days." On that day Mrs. Parks was convicted and fined for her offense. The Montgomery Improvement Association was organized to operate the protest and King was elected president. The boycott itself was nearly one hundred percent effective. But its nature and duration had still to be determined; that was left to the decision of a mass meeting in the evening, at which King was to deliver the main address. With only twenty minutes to prepare (he ordinarily spent fifteen hours in drafting a sermon), he went to the pulpit of the packed Holt Street Baptist Church without manuscript or notes and delivered what he termed the most decisive speech of his life. It was indeed decisive, for though King as yet made no conscious use of Gandhian ideas or terminology, his speech did combine in creative tension the core ideas of non-violent doctrine: an insistent demand for justice linked with an equally insistent rejection of hatred and violence as the path to justice. And its closing statement escalated its significance: "If you will protest courageously, and yet with dignity and Christian love, when the history books are written in future generations, the historians will have to pause and say, 'There lived a great people — a black people — who injected new meaning and dignity into the veins of civilization.' This is our challenge and our overwhelming responsibility." The speech drew a tumultuous response, and when the Reverend Ralph David Abernathy presented a resolution calling for continuance of the protest the assent was unanimous.

Because King thoroughly understood and fully meant what he said, the course of the movement was set from that moment. And for the same reasons he was able to keep it on that course in long bleak periods following frustrating and fruitless negotiations, at moments of near despair when the boycott faced defeat in biased courts and in times of threatening crisis such as the day his house was bombed. Ironically, the victory that finally came was not directly produced by the boycott but resulted from a separate legal action challenging the constitutionality of the city bus laws of Alabama. Without the federal courts and the lawyers of the National Association for the Advancement of Colored People, the movement might well have met final defeat. But it was the organization and sustenance of the protest that proved to Montgomery's Negroes their own resourcefulness and powers of endurance; a lesson not lost on black men elsewhere in the nation and the world. Most importantly, it was in the turmoil of the Montgomery protest that Martin Luther King brought his powers to maturity and shaped his theology of social change.

V Birmingham, Selma, Chicago: A Theology in Action

The Negro revolution of the 1950's and 1960's came to be identified with the story of Martin Luther King, Jr. A great deal went on within it in which he had no part and which had roots in events occurring before his entry to the scene. The revolution had other leaders who owed little or nothing to King's inspiration and who developed their own strategies and ideologies apart from him — leaders such as A. Philip Randolph, Malcolm X, Stokely Carmichael, Daisy Bates, Medgar Evers, James Farmer, Roy Wilkins, Whitney Young. Even in the ranks of King's SCLC there were men of great independent distinction, among them Ralph Abernathy, James Bevel, Andrew Young, Wyatt Tee Walker, Fred Shuttlesworth. In a limited sense King was bigger than the movement, in that he was the one figure to achieve world recognition and the one who was finally the most innovative of them all. But he was far from being the only mover and shaker, and despite his prominence he was never in a position to control or dominate the cause. Hence there is a built-in distortion in focusing solely on King in rehearsing the history of these times.

Another distortion results from remembering King exclusively in connection with the most dramatic events of his career — Montgomery, Birmingham, Selma, Chicago. Much of his influence was exerted in other, quieter ways; in sermons, speeches, essays, articles, interviews; in constant interchanges with his staff, in conferences with other civil rights figures, in negotiations with opposition forces and government officials. Although some of this influence was fleeting, a great part of it, including much that will never be traced to him, is permanently part of the American stream of consciousness.

With this understood it still remains true that such events as the Birmingham campaign showed King at his best, and that they have the most to say to us and to the future. It was King's development of non-violence that constituted his

most distinctive legacy, and it was principally through
action that he came to understand it. As he said many
times, he learned more from the experience of Montgomery
than from all the books on the subject he had ever read. The
same is true of the way in which his own teaching is
conveyed. Though he wrote lucidly about non-violence in
the abstract, the record of his campaigns is more instructive.
It is somewhat helpful to be told that the non-violent
strategist must be flexible and realistic; it is far more
illuminating to see King and his lieutenants advance,
retreat, adapt, invent under the pressure of reality. King
never attempted a definitive philosophical study of non-
violence, but he provided a casebook which every future
student will have to ponder.

What Gettysburg is to the military historian, Birmingham
will probably become to the historian of non-violence: a

classic campaign. It was a struggle for stated, significant yet limited goals. It engaged the masses of the Negro community in Birmingham and attracted the sympathy of most of the civilized world. Though planning occupied many months, in execution the campaign was compact and concentrated: the first sit-in took place April 3, 1963, the final agreement was signed May 10. From "moderates" and "neutrals" (in government, in the churches, even in the black community) came all the standard criticisms, all the classic arguments against choosing this time and this place to challenge injustice. The opposition used its every weapon, from court injunctions to massive brutality — thus confirming to the nation the diehard fanaticism with which the segregationists clung to their system, thereby multiplying the effect of the protest. When evil is pushed to the wall, it shows itself as evil and earns the rejection of mankind, provided the challenging forces do not confuse the issue by themselves resorting to hatred, retaliation, violence. That is the theory of non-violence. With King playing his usual role of uniting and inspiriting the protestors, and with Safety Commissioner "Bull" Connor providing invaluable assistance through his intransigent savagery, that was the lesson of Birmingham. Again, the story is worth reviewing in far more detail than can be included here, and again the best source is King's own account, given in *Why We Can't Wait.*

Selma, in 1965, was another victory, one in which the clergy of most denominations were represented in greater numbers than ever before. Albany, Georgia, in 1961-1962, was an instructive defeat (though not a total one), caused by failure to pinpoint the aims of the campaign. The Northern campaigns following Selma, such as the one in Chicago, brought partial victories, but none so dramatic or clear-cut as those in Alabama. Even now, however, it is premature to evaluate these efforts finally, for they are still having their effects. The same is true of the dozens of other drives initiated or endorsed by the SCLC, of hundreds that emulated King's methods and of the Poor People's Campaign planned before his death and carried on by his successors. If the record is taken as a whole, it demonstrates that non-violence has operational as well as theoretical validity, but that it demands courage, brains and timing.

VI White Liberals, Black Militants

Was King a "white man's Negro?"

Ten years before his death few would have dreamed of asking the question. As late as 1963 Robert F. Kennedy, then Attorney General, thought the Birmingham campaign ill timed — a euphemism suggesting it was too demanding, too pushy. And in the very month of his death a great many who thought of themselves as sympathizers with the black poor were saying that the Poor People's Campaign he was then planning was too dangerous, too disruptive, too ambitious.

Still, a curious transformation took place over the years; to threatened whites, he grew several shades paler. In television panel shows of the early period he occupied the ideological left, making such established figures as Roy Wilkins of the NAACP and Whitney Young of the Urban League seem respectable, if not domesticated. But when militants like Stokely Carmichael and Malcolm X, Rap Brown and Eldridge Cleaver made the scene, men who rejected non-violence and the love ethic and who said what they thought about Whitey, King began to be perceived as a moderate.

The change was in the situation, not in the man. If he was never a black nationalist, neither could he be called an accommodationist, an Uncle Tom. Even now no white liberal or middle-class escapee from the ghetto can read his indictment of their tepidity and feel comfortable. He understood that some whites could be for the movement only as long as they could patronize their Negro protégés, or until real trouble came, or until real sacrifice was asked; and he let them feel his scorn. He was expert in detecting hypocrisy and fence-straddling in politicians. He did not indulge in epithets, but his exposure of moral shame was nonetheless scathing. So far as issues are concerned, on none

of them did he compromise at any point short of full justice and equality. Nor did he become more manageable as he became more prestigious. On the contrary: Whereas his first target was desegregation of Montgomery's bus lines, at the end he was demanding an economic bill of rights with a price tag in the billions. And if white liberals couldn't accept such a program because it was just, he was willing to stuff it down their throats by means of mass non-violent action.

And yet there is something to be learned from black nationalists that cannot be learned from King, at least not as well. There were aspects of the misery of Negro existence which he knew from the outside — more intimately than a white man could, but not with the authority of experience. He could comprehend and even explain the absolute outrage, absolute alienation of the separatists, but he did not himself feel these emotions and his words did not have the piercing power of those who did. He was brought up in a middle class, if not exactly bourgeois family. His education made him a Western humanist; meaning not only that he was a man of reason but that he could not conceive of Western civilization in racial terms — what was good in it was not tainted for him by its whiteness. Finally, and most profoundly, he was Christian to the roots of his mind and heart. It was not in him to nurture hatred for even one white man, much less the white race.

Some black militants rejected King because of his advocacy of non-violence. To them it was a new way of toadying to the Man, of weighting the odds in Whitey's favor, of asking the slave to bend to the lash once more in reparation for the master's sins; it demanded inhuman heroism of the blacks to earn a modicum of human decency from whites. The fact that he was a clergyman — and to a degree visibly so, in intonation and mannerism — helped to discount his appeal for these militants. He might not be an Uncle Tom but he was "de Lawd." He was a leftover from the days when religion, for the blacks, was the only way of making reality tolerable and for whites a useful gimmick for keeping the slaves in their place.

But for others the core issue was not of means but of the goal: integration vs. apartheid. For the separatists integration was not only impossible but undesirable, wrong. White society was irreversibly corrupt; white middle class values were shallow and constricting; white racism was not an accident or an aberration but an expression of the sick white soul. Integration was just not worth fighting for: As James Baldwin put it, nobody wants to be integrated into a burning house. Finally, to set integration as the goal was to accept white standards and spurn your own — something you could only do on your knees, not on your feet.

Ironically, though King rejected black separatism, he helped make it possible. Seeing his achievements, one could filter out the Christian and Gandhian elements and concentrate on the color of the deed: Black men had made their own revolution. Not that King deprecated this consciousness: For him racial pride and confidence were not only practical tools of progress but absolute spiritual necessities. The Negro could not be a man as long as he was secretly ashamed of being a Negro, secretly convinced he could not compete in the white man's world. But for King, racial pride was not a destination but a way station on the road to full personhood. The black man who thought his blackness made him inferior was crippled; he would not be cured by thinking blackness made him better. It followed that integration of the races — true integration, not condescending white graciousness — was a necessity for integration of personalities, on both sides.

The rhetoric of black nationalism is shriller, but King believed his own vision was ultimately the more radical. He could and did argue that riots and the threat of riots were impractical as well as immoral — they would end by producing a fascist America. He could argue too that black separatism was not so much radical as romantic and parochial. When he persisted in singing "black and white together" as part of "We Shall Overcome," he was really saying that human nature was a good thing, that people can rise above their heritage and purify themselves of evil. A radical notion, indeed.

VII The Churches and the Status Quo

Standing on the deck of the battleship *Missouri* in Tokyo harbor, during the ceremonies marking the surrender of Japan and the end of World War II, General Douglas MacArthur surveyed the years filled with destruction and agony leading to that moment. The healing of the world, the building of peace, he said, had become in the atomic age a work of supereminent necessity; the first responsibility for its accomplishment lay with "the theologians." Presumably what he meant was that for the sake of survival men needed a fundamental new understanding of their relationships, and that in dealing with fundamentals men had to look to the experts on God.

The world's theologians no doubt agreed. If they responded adequately, the world did not recognize their wisdom. Some among them worked revolutions, temporary or lasting, in religious thought about religion. But despite a great striving after relevancy, only a few (Martin Buber, Dietrich Bonhoeffer, Reinhold Niebuhr, Teilhard de Chardin) succeeded in inserting fresh theological ideas into the consciousness of intellectuals. As for the masses, only one man, John XXIII, not himself a theologian by trade, seemed for a while able to revive among them a sense of aliveness and deep meaning in religion. But since his death the Catholic renewal has slowed and floundered. And the postwar Christian Democratic movement in Europe, born of the Resistance, achieved some social reforms but did not fulfill its transforming promise.

Should Martin Luther King be considered along with thinkers and movements like these, as conceivably an answer to MacArthur's hope?

In one sense he was not a theologian at all. His mature writings on religion are aimed at persuasion rather than analysis; at their deepest they are prophetic rather than creative. His theology was a synthesis, not a discovery. Moving out of a fundamentalist tradition, during his studies he acquired elements from the dominant rival schools in modern Protestant theology, liberalism and neo-orthodoxy, from the "social gospel" and from contemporary exis-

tentialism. Finally, from Gandhi and others he learned the meaning of non-violence. The resulting mixture was unique. The elements within it, however, were not original.

Yet King has been proposed as "the theologian for our time." The judgment comes from a perceptive theological analyst, Herbert Warren Richardson. Richardson grounds this appraisal in the goal King proposed as the end of all life, "the unity of persons in friendship," or "the total interrelatedness of man with man," and in his insistence on "non-violent striving to overcome evil with good" as the means demanded by the end. For Richardson this teaching constitutes a reformation of the Reformation and a doctrine peculiarly suited to coping in Christian fashion with an age of ideological conflict. It was not that King invented the ideas, but that they were the controlling elements in his thought and that they moved him to action. Without implying parity in stature between King and Karl Marx, there is a similarity; both believed it was necessary not only to understand the world but to change it. Only events to come will show whether King's insights are programmatically valid without the sustaining power of his presence. Yet it is no light thing to have perceived and put into practice a way of interpreting Christianity that makes it once more relevant and dynamic. Given the reach of King's influence, it is conceivable that MacArthur's challenge has found in him an answer.

It is a peculiarity of King's theology that much of it makes sense to non-Christians and non-theists; among those who marched with him and thought him the era's most significant leader were Jews, humanists, agnostics, religious skeptics, critics of the churches. Yet, to anyone who has read or heard his speeches and sermons, there is no doubting that his values, ideas and personality were fused with his religious faith. And he was not only a believer but a clergyman, willingly and proudly a professional servant of organized religion. At one point in the crisis of Selma, for example, he missed an important confrontation because he felt obliged to discharge his pulpit responsibilities in the Atlanta church where he was co-pastor with his father.

Yet King was also a candid critic of the church; what he said of other institutions in society he applied unsparingly to the institution of which he was a part, and his most frequent criticism dealt with the church's conformism. It was not the office of the church to endorse the social status quo, to reflect and make respectable the prevailing values of society. Among the institutions of the world, the church was the one which had to stand apart and pass judgment on society's norms — for it drew its own criteria from an independent source. The world is always at odds with the scriptural ideals of justice and charity; it needs to be moved rather than soothed. Yet the church, accepting those ideals as its own, was too often the world's comforter rather than its affliction. The most obvious examples of its failure were slavery and segregation; by ignoring or excusing these radical and cruel injustices the church had violated its inner being. Worse yet: The churches not only condoned segregation but practiced it, even offered godly arguments in its support. And it did not stop there. The church was responsible also for the complacency of Christians toward war and poverty. It always counseled charity toward the "unfortunate," but it was blind to injustice, and for the church this was a deep sin of betrayal — for it had been both commissioned and equipped to discern the presence of injustice and to cry out against it.

Inevitably, this kind of criticism rankled. The response of "respectable" churchmen is forever enshrined in the unfortunate statement published by high-ranking clergymen of Alabama during the testing of Birmingham, the statement that drew from King his "Letter from Birmingham Jail." The statement is as much a classic, in its way, as was King's magnificent reply. But other churchmen, lay and clerical, reacted differently. It was, after all, among believing religionists of both races that King found his base of power. The extent to which churchmen accepted his critique of the church and his understanding of its mission was most vividly in evidence at Selma, where ministers, priests, nuns and even bishops put their bodies on the line with his. His appeal reached high into the bureaucracy of the Protestant churches, it furnished a rationale for men like Milwaukee's Father James Groppi, and many a congregational battle was fought over his name. Even now, though his doctrine of love and non-violence can be separated from the religious faith which fueled it for King, it seems safe to say that the future of his influence lies chiefly with the churches — or, at least, with religious minded men and women. The question is whether he will be ensconced in a martyr's shrine or accepted still as a leader of men, an active model for the anointed of God.

Thomas Harris

VIII Speak Truth to Power:

The War and the Movement

King's opposition to the war in Vietnam is more significant for what it says about King than for its effect on the conduct of the war or on the state of American public opinion. This is not to say that his position was regarded lightly or had no impact. The peace movement welcomed him to its platforms — not surprisingly, since by the time he became outspoken against the war his stature was such that he was the most prestigious non-political figure in the country ever to join its ranks. But his involvement in the anti-war movement was primarily verbal and relatively restrained. He did not lead in the application of direct action techniques to the Vietnam issue; although he sanctioned conscientious objection, he did not endorse draft resistance or other forms of civil disobedience. Moreover, in the public mind he was thoroughly identified with the cause he led, so that his authority in civil rights was not automatically transferable to issues of war and peace. Beyond doubt, the mere fact of King's stand on the war, together with the reasons he gave for condemning it, opened the consciences of some of his followers, white and black. Equally beyond doubt, his influence was less than decisive.

He must have known that this would be the case. He must have known, too, that he was risking a loss of personal prestige, withdrawal of support from the SCLC, creation of a split in the civil rights movement, angry denunciation from the President and a cooling of pro-Negro sentiment in Congress. To one extent or another, all these possible risks were realized in the event. There was criticism even from the sources (e.g., the *New York Times)* that were dubious about the war as well as strongly sympathetic toward King. The verdict of *Time* magazine in its obituary notice bespoke the conventional wisdom in its suggestion that King had diffused his impact by stepping out from his role in civil rights.

It is arguable that there were elements of unconscious racism in such judgments, leading to a serious misreading of King's whole character and consequently of his mission. One cannot imagine the *Times'* holding that a pediatrician like Benjamin Spock, a psychiatrist like Erich Fromm, a novelist like Mary McCarthy or a poet like Robert Lowell was not free to voice his conscience-born condemnation of the war, or to expose its malign influence on the nation's mental and spiritual health. Yet when King pointed out the disastrous effect of the vast expenditures in Vietnam on programs for social renewal in the U.S., when he questioned the order of priorities involved, when he applied to the war the same moral standards he had brought to bear on segregation, he was accused of misusing his leadership and of confusing issues.

What King's stand on the war says of him is that he was not to be captured within categories determined by tradition or the mass media or the practical politics of minority-group maneuvering. Just as he had ripped open the silk curtain surrounding the ministry, so also he broke through the limitations tacitly imposed on the black civil rights leader. He could never be a professional Negro any more than he would be a professional religionist. He was a man before he was a black man, and God's prophet before he was the church's agent.

In his critique of the war King was careful to keep in perspective arguments drawn from the war's effect on the black poor and from its violation of his own belief in non-violence. True, he spoke with special vividness of the irony of sending young black men across the Pacific "to guarantee liberties in Southeast Asia which they had not found in Southwest Georgia and East Harlem," and of the further irony of the nation's spending $322,000 in Vietnam for each enemy killed while allotting $53 for each person in America classified as poor. But this aspect of the war was one of many included in his judgment, and not even the commanding one. He condemned also the militarism expressed in the war policy, its unspoken acceptance of neo-colonialism, its arrogant jingoism and obsessional anti-communism. Just as in working for Negro emancipation he used his knowledge of history, sociology and democratic theory, so also in his judgment of the war he incorporated his sound grasp of its historical and geo-political context. In all the literature of the Vietnam protest there can have been few more sweepingly inclusive indictments than King's address of April 4, 1967, at Riverside Church in New York City.

As for his belief in non-violence, it served as the crown rather than the foundation of his argument. Despite the awful risks mankind had imposed on itself by the development of nuclear and chemical weapons in an era of tense ideological conflict, he knew that non-violence was simply not developed to the point where its application to international conflict would seem a credible option. So his argument led up to but did not depend on his ultimate belief. If the U.S. was not mature enough to abandon its trust in military power, at least it could be decent. If the time was not opportune for the full establishment of the structure of peace, at least a prophet of peace could stand up among his own people and denouce a particularly futile and vicious war.

If King's success in life were to be estimated by means of opinion polls and the other indicators so much valued in contemporary journalism (valued because they allow the substitution of measurement for judgment), then it would have to be accepted that he reduced his immediate effectiveness, strained some of his alliances, gained many new enemies and acquired few new admirers by giving voice to his view on the war. Before the anniversary of his death, however, it was clear that in any longer term perspective what he said and did about the war confirmed the large dimensions of his spirit.

IX Free at Last: Memphis

Any man who lays down his life for his friend gives the final proof of love. Not many among the world's millions are called on to supply that proof, but even among the select few who have done so there are kinds and degrees of heroism. There are heroes in bad causes, who die not for the cause but to save their comrades. There are heroes who respond instantly to the urgent call of the moment — like the soldier who falls on a live grenade to shield his buddies, there are others who routinely accept sustained high risk to rescue men in peril. In our time those who gain or even seek the power of office know that the very quest makes them vulnerable: witness the deaths of John and Robert Kennedy. And history records also the special martyrdom suffered by men like Thomas More, who give up life rather than give up conscience, who decide their own fate in loneliness and without even the support of seeing how their courage will serve others, who die in ultimate cool devotion to integrity.

For Martin Luther King, death by violence was not, in the strict sense, inevitable. But it was highly probable, and he knew it. He could hardly escape knowing it. Almost daily from the outset of the Montgomery boycott we heard the ugliest of threats, and within weeks the reality of their venom was made credible with the first bombing of his home. A steel letter opener driven into his chest by a deranged woman in New York came within centimeters of being fatal. Even without these cruel reminders, there was evidence of the risk: the deaths of Jimmy Lee Jackson and the Reverend James J. Reeb, of four little girls in the bombing of a Birmingham church, of Medgar Evers and three civil rights workers in Mississippi, the attack on James Meredith, the assassination of President Kennedy.

He was a specialist in love but a realist about hatred. He believed that goodness was more powerful than evil and that it would overcome — but only "some day." Meantime evil had its own power, and victory would have its price. He fully expected that his own life would be part of the price. In the war on racism he had become so great a symbol that wherever he was, there was the front line. To be effective he had to be exposed, vulnerable. He could not and would not have accepted either the degree of isolation or the amount of protection a President could have — and even a President, as John Kennedy knew, could not be really safe from a determined killer. Kennedy accepted the risk with cool stoicism. King did more. He did not want to die, but he embraced his fate beforehand and offered it as part of the

redemptive suffering necessary to heal humanity. It was never more apparent than in the sermon he gave in Memphis on the eve of his assassination how fully he had conquered fear, how frankly and unflinchingly he had looked on the face of death.

Scant hours after the killing, a United States Senator said he was sorry to learn of it, but not surprised. Martin Luther King had been killed, he said, because he was always "stickin' his nose in other people's business."

The Senator from Louisiana was right, of course. This time the other people were the garbage workers of Memphis, who were being cheated of a decent wage and denied means to better their lot. It was because King made their weakness his concern that he was shot, the blood gushed out, he died.

It was an ugly way to die, a savage, crude denial of his life's theme. It was endlessly saddening, a crime nearly beyond forgiveness. But it was not random and senseless. He lived to bring justice to poor black men and women. It was a good cause to die for.

X Final Tributes

The murder elicited strong, varied emotions. Out of fear, police were alerted and troops mobilized; the President called for calm. Fear rose because everyone knew anger would rise — one more black leader had been eliminated because he could not be silenced. And anger did speak: In dozens of cities there was burning and looting or the threat of it. There was also despair among blacks, and for some a final conversion to cynicism.

But along with these there was honest, deep grief, among at least some whites and among millions of blacks; and there was the response King himself would have hoped for, a conscious, willed rejection of hatred, a renewal of the beliefs he had imparted.

In that turbulent week, the one person who best told the truth about Martin Luther King and his death, the one who most simply and profoundly summed up the meaning of his life was the woman who had already sacrificed her life with him for the cause he led. Many said that in the nobility of her bearing she recalled the incredible valor of Jacqueline Kennedy in the prolonged moments of anguish after Dallas. But Coretta King was called upon to do more. It was she who authenticated for the freedom movement and the greater public the transfer of leadership from her fallen husband to Ralph Abernathy. And it was she who could speak with the authority of her personal grief to his outraged followers, asking them to forgive the unforgivable, to remain true to his ethic of love though hatred had triumphed over his body. In the midst of awful shock she demonstrated that she had been as ready as he for the blow to fall. Her intelligence functioned as well as her character; her brief statement, written and delivered only brief hours later, not only gave him perfect tribute but pointed the way to continuance of his work:

> *"He knew that at any moment his physical life could be cut short, and we faced this possibility squarely and honestly. My husband faced this possibility of death without bitterness or hatred. . . . He gave his life for the poor of the world — the garbage workers of Memphis and the peasants of Vietnam. Nothing hurt him more than that man could attempt no way to solve problems except through violence. He gave his life in search of a more excellent way, a creative rather than a destructive way. We intend to go on in search of that way, and I hope that you who loved and admired him would join us in fulfilling his dream.*

Thomas Harris

By that standard most other responses fell short — as those who gave them knew they would. But the President, the Pope, the official eulogists, the hundreds of thousands of mourners in Atlanta did succeed in registering to the world their awareness of the man's stature. If their words did not always rise to the occasion, there was no doubt of the depth and sincerity of their feelings. The cruel assassin, in the immediate aftermath of his crime, achieved something of what must have been his larger purpose: There was a new chasm between whites and blacks. But because Martin Luther King was the kind of man he was, there was still hope of healing. To many blacks his death was convincing final proof of white perfidy, yet it was still possible to appeal against this verdict because he would not have accepted it. And for those whites who had taken him as their own leader, it was at last possible to know what it was like to be robbed of leadership by violence.

It is the theme of this book that the final summing up of Martin Luther King's life cannot yet be made. In the aftermath of his death many vows were spoken, in public and in private, that his work would go on. Those vows are still being tested. As prophet and martyr, he was a gift to the nation. We have yet to show if we deserved the gift.

Reflections

This chapter exists because there are a few more things to be said. It should acknowledge, first, that the editor's contributions to this volume do not succeed in evoking again the grief imposed by the assassin. That is a fault, for grief has its uses. For a white middle-class American, it is more useful to feel real grief over one black man's death rather than generalized guilt toward all black men. In that moment we learned that what we felt for Martin Luther King was more than respect or admiration. Despite his public reserve and clerical dignity, he inspired personal devotion, even among people who had never met him or seen him face to face. Knowing we would never again be lifted by his words, we found we had loved him. The sharpness of that first pain is gone. It is worth recalling for ourselves because, however terrible the occasion, it was a good discovery. It is worth recording for the future as well. No one who has not lived in his time will quite grasp how he came to be so great a symbol of man's nobility; at least we can authenticate for posterity that it was not only his cause but his person that lived in our hearts.

Our present problem is that we still need him, and not just his ideas. It is one of the great cliches of our era — so often said that it draws only a sigh even from those who fully grasp it — that man's spiritual and moral progress has not kept up with his scientific and technological advances. However trite, it is still true, and ominously so in an age when obliteration is an available alternative. In this dangerous time King was one of very few human beings whose presence gave some reason to hope for the kind of radical change of heart the world needs. It would be silly to maintain that his spirit prevailed; but then he had so little time to work. His murderer — perhaps fortunately for his own sanity — will never understand what it was he killed.

It is only realism to acknowledge that we need his presence as well as his thought. Pre-eminently this is a time of conflict, and what King devised was a spirituality of conflict, a technique for overcoming evil without being overcome by it. His idea was a radically simple one, and derivative; but it took a degree of genius to make it work. And not only genius, but unlimited faith.

In the absence of that genius, gifted with only moderate shares of faith, our hope must be that apprentices can follow where the master has shown the way. Surprising people speak now of non-violence as a way of life — a black U. S. congressman, a beautiful folk-singer, a Brazilian archbishop, an anti-Franco Catalonian. True, in the very year of his death, and partly because of his death, the polarization of races and of ideological groupings escalated; revolution, not non-violence, was the avant-garde fad. But permanence is built into King's doctrine precisely because its central element, love as a weapon, was borrowed from a greater source. He was not a sage who proclaimed a new truth, but a prophet who renewed an old one.

Excerpts from Writings and Speeches of Martin Luther King, Jr.

... I had almost despaired of the power of love in solving social problems. The "turn the other cheek" and the "love your enemies" philosophy are only valid, I felt, when individuals are in conflict with other individuals; when racial groups and nations are in conflict a more realistic approach is necessary. Then I came upon the life and teachings of Mahatma Gandhi. As I read his works I became deeply fascinated by his campaigns of non-violent resistance. The whole Gandhian concept of *satyagraha* (*satya* is truth which equals love, and *graha* is force; *satyagraha* thus means truth-force or love-force) was profoundly significant to me. As I delved deeper into the philosophy of Gandhi my skepticism concerning the power of love gradually diminished, and I came to see for the first time that the Christian doctrine of love operating through the Gandhian method of nonviolence was one of the most potent weapons available to oppressed people in their struggle for freedom.

"Pilgrimage to Nonviolence," *The Christian Century* (April 13, 1960)

Robert Fitch (Black Star)

The far-reaching solutions for lifting the "weight of centuries" will necessarily involve systematic liquidation of ghetto life, loans and grants to provide equal opportunities for the unequally equipped, adult education, remedial clinics for damaged families and individuals and integrated housing construction on a scale commensurate with the extent of slums, rather than with the extent of budgets.

"In A Word—Now," *New York Times Magazine* (September 29, 1963)

We have learned in the course of our freedom struggle that the needs of 20 million Negroes are not truly separable from those of nearly 200 million whites and Negroes in America, all of whom will benefit from a color-blind land of plenty. . . . Our vote would place in Congress true representatives of the people who would legislate for the Medicare, housing, schools and jobs required by all men of any color.

"Civil Right No. 1—The Right to Vote," *New York Times Magazine* (March 14, 1965)

At the end of the Selma to Montgomery march for civil rights, Dr. and Mrs. King rested on the courthouse steps.

Our nation was born in genocide when it embraced the doctrine that the original American, the Indian, was an inferior race. . . . We are perhaps the only nation which tried as a matter of national policy to wipe out its indigenous population. Moreover, we elevated that tragic experience into a noble crusade. . . .

Our children are still taught to respect the violence which reduced a red-skinned people of an earlier culture into a few fragmented groups herded into impoverished reservations. . . .

WHY WE CAN'T WAIT

During the 1963 March on Washington, King spoke from the Lincoln Memorial to the nation "born in genocide."

58

If this [nonviolent] philosophy had not emerged, by now many streets of the South would, I am convinced, be flowing with blood. And I am further convinced that if our white brothers dismiss as "rabble-rousers" and "outside agitators" those of us who employ nonviolent direct action, and if they refuse to support our nonviolent efforts, millions of Negroes will, out of frustration and despair, seek solace and security in black-nationalist ideologies — a development that would inevitably lead to a frightening racial nightmare.
LETTER FROM BIRMINGHAM JAIL

Many people believe that the urban Negro is too angry and too sophisticated to be nonviolent. Those same people dismiss the nonviolent marches in the South and try to describe them as processions of pious elderly ladies. The fact is that in all the marches we have organized, some men of very violent tendencies have been involved. It was routine for us to collect hundreds of knives from our own ranks before the demonstrations, in case of momentary weakness.
"Next Stop: The North," *Saturday Review* (November 13, 1965)

Protest in Grenada, Mississippi, in the fall of 1966 — something more than "processions of pious elderly ladies."

Robert Fitch (Black Star)

Robert Fitch (Black Star)

Leading the resistance into the streets, King, here with Reverend
Andrew Young, demanded the government take a stand.

64

Birmingham 1963: making injustice known.

Ivan Massar (Black Star)

Last Sunday more than 8,000 of us started on a mighty walk from Selma, Alabama. We have walked on meandering highways and rested our bodies on rocky byways. Some of our faces are burned from the outpourings of the sweltering sun. Some have literally slept in the mud. We have been drenched by the rains. . . .

They told us we wouldn't get here. And there were those who said that we would get here [Montgomery] only over their dead bodies, but all the world today knows that we are here and that we are standing before the forces of power in the state of Alabama saying, "We ain't goin' let nobody turn us around."

State Capitol Building, Montgomery, Alabama, at the end of the march from Selma to Montgomery
(*New York Times*, March 26, 1965)

King confronted the State of Alabama's forces once again at the capital, Montgomery, in 1965.

The most grievous charge against municipal police is not brutality, though it exists. Permissive crime in ghettos is designed, directed, and cultivated by white national crime syndicates operating numbers, narcotics, and prostitution rackets freely in the protected sanctuaries of the ghettos. Because no one, including the police, cares particularly about ghetto crime, it pervades every area of life. The Negro child who learns too little about books in his pathetic schools, learns too much about crime in the streets around him. Even when he and his family resist its corruption, its presence is a source of fear and of moral debilitation.

"Next Stop: The North," *Saturday Review* (November 13, 1965)

With his own daughters, Yolanda and Bernice in mind, King knew no black man has escaped the pressure of the ghetto: "Even when he [the Negro] and his family resist its corruption, its presence is a source of fear and moral debilitation."

Last summer our own children lived with us in Lawn-dale (a Chicago slum), and it was only a few days before we became aware of the change in their behavior. Their tempers flared and they sometimes reverted to almost infantile behavior. As riots raged around them outside, I realized that the crowded flat in which we lived was about to produce an emotional explosion in my own family. It was just too hot, too crowded, too devoid of creative forms of recreation. There was just not space enough in the neighborhood to run off the energy of childhood without running into busy, traffic-laden streets. And I understood anew the conditions which make of the ghetto an emotional pressure cooker.
WHERE DO WE GO FROM HERE

King and Bernice during a pleasant moment in their Atlanta home.

While I lay in that quiet front bedroom, with a distant street lamp throwing a reassuring glow through the curtained window, I began to think of the viciousness of people who would bomb my home. I could feel the anger rising when I realized that my wife and baby could have been killed. I thought about the city commissioners and all the statements they had made about me and the Negro generally. I was once more on the verge of corroding hatred. And once more I caught myself and said: "You must not allow yourself to become bitter."
STRIDE TOWARD FREEDOM

If I meet hate with hate, I become depersonalized, because creation is so designed that my personality can only be fulfilled in the context of community. Booker T. Washington was right: "Let no man pull you so low as to make you hate him." When he pulls you that low he brings you to the point of working against community; he drags you to the point of defying creation, and thereby becoming depersonalized.
"Pilgrimage to Nonviolence"
  The Christian Century (April 13, 1960)

Martin Luther King III with his father — a man fulfilled only in the context of community.

Who are we? We are the descendants of slaves. We are the offspring of noble men and women who were kidnapped from their native land and chained in ships like beasts. We are the heirs of a great and exploited continent known as Africa. We are the heirs of a past of rope, fire and murder. I for one am not ashamed of this past. My shame is for those who became so inhuman that they could inflict this torture upon us.

WHERE DO WE GO FROM HERE

Feeling shame for those who attacked schoolmates of these children in Grenada, Mississippi, King upheld "the heirs of a past of rope, fire and murder."

Somewhere there has to be a synthesis. I have to be militant enough to satisfy the militant, yet I have to keep enough discipline in the movement to satisfy white supporters and moderate Negroes.

It puts me in a difficult position.

New York Times (July 17, 1966) from an interview in Chicago, Illinois

I still believe in nonviolence, and no one is going to turn me around on that point. If every Negro in the United States turns to violence, I am going to stand up and be the only voice to say that it is wrong.

United Baptist Church, Montclair, New Jersey
(*New York Times*, September 12, 1966)

Selma 1965: "No one is going to turn me around. . . ."

Steve Schapiro (Black Star)

77

Vernon Merritt III (Black Star)

Good still has a way of growing out of evil. The blood of these girls must serve a revitalizing force to bring light to this dark city.

Tribute at funeral services for four girls killed in
Birmingham, Alabama, church bombing
(*New York Times*, September 19, 1963)

We will match your capacity to inflict suffering with our capacity to endure suffering. We will meet your physical force with soul force. We will not hate you, but we cannot in all good conscience obey your unjust laws. . . . But we will soon wear you down by our capacity to suffer. And in winning our freedom, we will so appeal to your heart and conscience that we will win you in the process.

"Dr. King, Symbol of the Segregation Struggle,"
New York Times Magazine (January 22, 1961)

One wounded affects us all.

. . . I believe that wounded justice, lying prostrate on the blood-flowing streets of our nations, can be lifted from this dust of shame to reign supreme among the children of men.

Acceptance of 1964 Nobel Peace Prize, Oslo, Norway
(*New York Times*, December 11, 1964)

. . . All life is inter-related. Whatever affects one of us, affects all.

Address to Students at Oslo University, Oslo, Norway
(*New York Times*, December 12, 1964)

As early as 1958, King grew with the conviction that unearned suffering is redemptive.

Due to my involvement in the struggle for the freedom of my people, I have known very few quiet days in the last few years. I have been arrested five times and put in Alabama jails. My home has been bombed twice. A day seldom passes that my family and I are not the recipients of threats of death. . . .

. . . Recognizing the necessity for suffering I have tried to make of it a virtue. If only to save myself from bitterness, I have attempted to see my personal ordeals as an opportunity to transform myself and heal the people involved in the tragic situation which now obtains. I have lived these last few years with the conviction that unearned suffering is redemptive.

"Suffering and Faith," *The Christian Century* (April 27, 1960)

. . . I had hoped that the white moderate would understand that the present tension in the South is a necessary phase of the transition from an obnoxious negative peace, in which the Negro passively accepted his unjust plight, to a substantive and positive peace, in which all men will respect the dignity and worth of human personality. Actually, we who engage in nonviolent direct action are not the creators of tension. We merely bring to the surface the hidden tension that is already alive.

LETTER FROM BIRMINGHAM JAIL

King's non-violent opposition grew with the transition from a negative peace and with his 1958 arrest in Montgomery.

Charles Moore (Black Star)

He continued to bring the tension to the surface, notably during his 1963 Birmingham jailing.

I still believe that love is the most durable power in the world. Over the centuries men have sought to discover the highest good. This has been the chief quest of ethical philosophy. . . . What is the summum bonum of life? . . . It is love. This principle stands at the center of the cosmos. As John says, "God is love." He who loves is a participant in the being of God. He who hates does not know God.

"The Most Durable Power," *The Christian Century* (June 5, 1957)

. . . Someone must have sense enough and morality enough to cut off the chain of hate. This can be done only by projecting the ethics of love to the center of our lives.

"Nonviolence and Racial Justice," *The Christian Century* (February 6, 1957)

Towards a positive peace: at home in his Atlanta church.

88

Whenever you take a stand for truth and justice, you are liable to scorn. Often you will be called an impractical idealist or a dangerous radical. Sometimes it might mean going to jail. If such is the case you must honorably grace the jail with your presence. It might even mean physical death. But if physical death is the price that some must pay to free their children from a permanent life of psychological death, then nothing could be more Christian.

I still believe that standing up for the truth of God is the greatest thing in the world. This is the end of life. The end of life is not to be happy. The end of life is not to achieve pleasure and avoid pain. The end of life is to do the will of God, come what may.

"The Most Durable Power," *The Christian Century* (June 5, 1957)

If "physical death is the price some must pay to free their children,"
both King and his son, Martin Luther III, were prepared for that event.

I have the audacity to believe that peoples everywhere can have three meals a day for their tired bodies, education and culture for their minds, and dignity, equality and freedom for their spirits. I believe that what self-centered men have torn down, men other-centered can build up. I still believe that one day mankind will bow before the altars of God and be crowned triumphant over war and bloodshed, and nonviolent redemptive goodwill will proclaim the rule of the land. "And the lion and the lamb shall lie down together and every man shall sit under his own vine and fig tree and none shall be afraid." I still believe that we shall overcome.

Acceptance of 1964 Nobel Peace Prize, Oslo, Norway
(*New York Times,* December 11, 1964)

"I have the audacity to believe . . . that peoples everywhere can have . . . equality and freedom for their spirits."

Robert Fitch (Black Star)

Always be sure that you struggle with Christian methods and Christian weapons. Never succumb to the temptation of becoming bitter. As you press on for justice, be sure to move with dignity and discipline, using only the weapon of love. ... If you succumb to the temptation of using violence in your struggle, unborn generations will be the recipients of a long and desolate night of bitterness, and your chief legacy to the future will be an endless reign of meaningless chaos.

"The Most Durable Power," *The Christian Century* (June 5, 1957)

Coretta King, in the days following the assassination, moved "with dignity and discipline, using only the weapon of love. . . ."

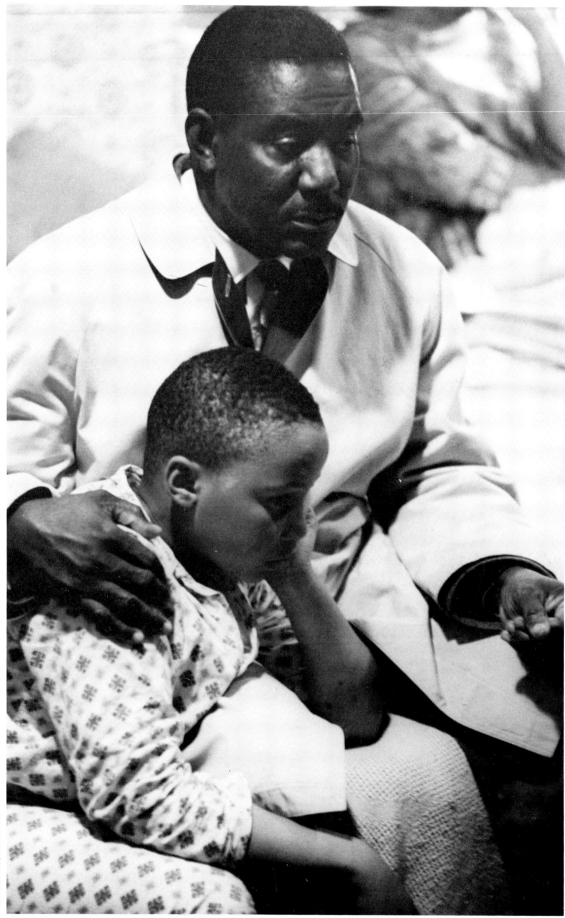

Robert Fitch (Black Star)

94

Not every minister can be a prophet, but some must be prepared for the ordeals of this high calling and be willing to suffer courageously for righteousness. May the problem of race in America soon make hearts burn so that prophets will rise up, saying, "Thus saith the Lord," and cry out as Amos did, ". . . let justice roll down like waters, and righteousness like an ever-flowing stream."

"The Church and the Race Crisis," *The Christian Century* (October 8, 1958) (published with permission from STRIDE TOWARD FREEDOM)

There is no price in the world too great to pay for freedom.

Zion's Chapel Methodist Church, Marion, Alabama (*The New York Times*, February 23, 1965)

"If you succumb to the temptation of using violence in your struggle, unborn generations will be the recipients of a long and desolate night of bitterness. . . ."

Robert Fitch (Black Star)

[My husband] never hated. He never despaired of well doing. And he encouraged us to do likewise, and so he prepared us constantly for the tragedy.

I am surprised and pleased at the success of his teaching, for our children say calmly, "Daddy is not dead; he may be physically dead, but his spirit will never die."

. . . He gave his life in search of a more excellent way, a more effective way, a creative rather than a destructive way.

We intend to go on in search of that way, and I hope that you who loved and admired him would join us in fulfilling his dream.

Statement by Mrs. Martin Luther King, Jr., at
the Ebenezer Baptist Church in Atlanta, April 6, 1968

"We intend to go on in search of that way. . . ." — Coretta King, April 1968